SUPERSTAR PLANTS

Louise Spilsbury

PowerKiDS press™

New York

Published in 2015 by The Rosen Publishing Group
29 East 21st Street, New York, NY 10010

Produced for Rosen by Calcium Creative Ltd
Editor for Calcium Creative Ltd: Sarah Eason
US Editor: Joshua Shadowens
Designer: Paul Myerscough

Photo credits: Cover: Shutterstock: Sarin Kunthong (left), Marco Uliana (top), Andreas Zerndl
(right). Inside: Dreamstime: Ajimns 1, 8, Andreas Altenburger 9b, April21st 27b, Burtct
19t, Gemsbok 11t, Hadkhanong 27t, Koon Hong Kang 20, Tamara Kulikova 5t, Mwicks 6,
Pierdelune 7t, Pindiyath100 11b, Raomn 7b, Sikth 10; Shutterstock: Antpkr 16, Beboy 23t,
Jez Bennett 13b, Darren J. Bradley 22, Adisorn Chaisan 17t, Ethan Daniels 18, G2019 9t,
Gitanna 4, Martin Good 28–29, Charles Harker 25b, Mykhailo Kalinskyi 18b, Kletr 15b,
Sarin Kunthong 21t, Martha Marks 13t, K. Miri Photography 2–3, 17b, Natashamam 29t,
Nazzu 12, Dean Pennala 23b, Raulbaenacasado 15t, Teerapun 26, Wildnerdpix 21b, Anke
van Wyk 24, Vladislavs Zarovs 25t, Andreas Zerndl 14, Oleg Znamenskiy 5b; Wikimedia
Commons: Dysmorodrepanis, Own photo, Cologne University Botanical Collection 28.

Library of Congress Cataloging-in-Publication Data

Spilsbury, Louise.
  Superstar plants / by Louise Spilsbury.
      pages cm. — (Nature's got talent)
Includes index.
ISBN 978-1-4777-7072-6 (library binding) — ISBN 978-1-4777-7073-3 (pbk.) —
ISBN 978-1-4777-7074-0 (6-pack)
1. Plants—Miscellanea—Juvenile literature. 2. Curiosities and wonders—Juvenile literature. I.
Title. II. Series: Nature's got talent.
QK50.S65 2015
580—dc 3
                                    2014003094

Manufactured in the United States of America

CPSIA Compliance Information: Batch #WS14PK7: For Further Information contact Rosen Publishing, New York, New York at 1-800-237-9932

Contents

Plants   4

Giant Redwood   6

Rafflesia   8

Venus Flytrap   10

Baobab Tree   12

Bee Orchid   14

Bamboo   16

Coconut   18

Giant Amazon Water Lily   20

Bristlecone Pine   22

Mesquite Tree   24

Jackfruit Tree   26

Amazing Adaptations   28

Glossary   30

Further Reading   31

Websites   31

Index   32

Plants

Mosses on a damp rock, cacti in a desert, crops in a field, and mighty trees in a forest are very different, but they are all plants. There are around 330,000 different types of plant worldwide! All of these distinct plant types have several features in common.

All plants make their own food by the process of photosynthesis. This process uses sunlight to change carbon dioxide gas from air and water into sugar.

Most leaves are green because they contain a green substance called chlorophyll, which is used for photosynthesis.

Most plants make **seeds** that they make in flowers or in **cones**.

Most plants have roots, **stems**, and leaves.

Plant Superstars

All plants are amazing, but some are more astonishing than others! In this book we are going to find out about some of the world's most talented plant superstars.

Secret Stars

The dragon's blood tree gets its name from the bright red **sap** that oozes from its trunk when it is cut. The sap protects the plant from infection. It has also been used by people as lipstick, violin varnish, and even for magic potions!

5

Giant Redwood

The champion plant for height is the giant redwood. These huge trees regularly grow 350 feet (106 m) tall. The tallest specimen reaches 380 feet (116 m) high, which is taller than the Statue of Liberty. This redwood is so tall that its top branches trap fog!

The branches of the redwood are often 5 feet (1.5 m) thick.

Redwoods are named for the red-colored bark on the outside of the trees and wood inside.

Redwood roots grow mostly near the surface of the forest floor, where it is covered with fallen leaves and bark. The roots take up **nutrients** from the leaves and bark.

GENERAL SHERMAN

Secret Stars

Giant redwoods have some equally enormous relatives called giant sequoias. The largest living thing on Earth is a giant sequoia named General Sherman. Although just 275 feet (84 m) tall, it is 102 feet (31 m) around its base and weighs 2.7 million pounds (1.2 million kg).

Survival Tactics

Giant redwoods can live for hundreds of years. They have very thick bark that helps protect the wood inside from damage when there are forest fires. Their roots, which can measure hundreds of miles (km) in total, seek water and nutrients for the tree.

Although giant redwood cones are just 1 inch (2.5 cm) long, enormous new trees may grow from the tiny seeds inside.

7

Rafflesia

Compared to a delicate rose, the *Rafflesia* flower is a true monster of a plant! This enormous flower weighs 15 pounds (7 kg) and is 3 feet (1 m) wide. When the plant is about to flower, it develops a swelling that looks a little like a red cabbage. The flower opens for only a few days before withering.

The *Rafflesia* has no leaves because it does not make its own food. Instead, it steals nutrients from the vines on which it lives.

The thick, fleshy lobes of the *Rafflesia* flower are reddish-brown with white, raised spots.

The flower's central hole conceals the parts inside that produce berries with tiny seeds.

Corpse Flower

An appalling smell in a Southeast Asian forest might not be a dead animal but, instead, the foul perfume of a *Rafflesia* flower! The plant uses its strong smell to attract flies to its flower. The flies **pollinate** the flowers, which then make seeds that produce more *Rafflesias*.

Pollen sticks to flies visiting a *Rafflesia* flower. They may carry the pollen to another flower in their search for food.

Secret Stars

The titan arum is the largest flower spike in the world. It produces a 6-feet- (2-m-) tall spike surrounded by a 9-feet- (3-m-) wide crimson frill. The insects that pollinate this plant are attracted to the smell made by the thousands of flowers on the spike when it heats up.

9

Venus Flytrap

The Venus flytrap is a very unusual plant. It gets most of the nutrients it needs from soil and air, but it also uses its leaves to trap and kill unsuspecting insects. Juices it makes inside its leaves **digest** the soft parts of the insect, breaking it down into useful nutrients. The plant then spits out the insect's exoskeleton.

When the stiff hairs on the leaves of a Venus flytrap are touched, the two halves of the leaf close together.

The fly-catching part of the leaf is at the top of another, seemingly ordinary leaf.

Spines on the edge of the leaf interlock when it closes, forming an insect-trapping cage.

Fast But Fussy

Venus flytraps close their leaves in a fraction of a second after an insect touches them. The leaves do not immediately close up tight so tiny insects can escape through the spines. These little bugs are not much of a meal!

It takes a Venus flytrap up to 12 days to digest a fly.

Secret Stars

Venus flytraps are not the only plants that feed on animals. Pitcher plants have leaf tips that are shaped like socks with trap doors. Animals, such as insects and mice, which visit the plant in search of sweet **nectar**, drown in the liquid inside. Chemicals in the liquid digest the animals and the pitcher plant absorbs their nutrients.

Baobab Tree

The baobab tree, found in hot places such as East Africa, has a massive trunk topped with short branches. It looks as if the tree has been planted upside down! Its most remarkable talent is swelling up with water during the rainy season. This supply of water keeps the tree alive during the long, hot season.

The trunk of the baobab has folds that are most obvious in the dry season. The folds smooth as the trunk swells after rain has fallen.

Baobab bark is thick and full of fibers. It does not burn even during natural local fires.

Secret Stars

Cacti also swell up after rainfall. The giant saguaro cactus is the largest type, reaching 67 feet (20 m) tall. It droops and wrinkles when there is no rain. After it rains, the plant can store tons (t) of water in readiness for the dry season.

Tree of Plenty

Baobabs are trees of plenty. For example, elephants eat the sweet, white powder in the tree's fruit. As the elephants eat the fruit, they also eat its seeds. The seeds are then scattered in the elephants' dung. New baobab trees may then grow. Elephants also strip and eat the tree's bark in dry periods in order to absorb the water inside the bark. However, the baobab tree easily regrows new bark.

Baobab trees can survive elephant damage. They remain alive even if half their trunk is missing!

13

Bee Orchid

Is it a bee or is it a flower? It is both! The bee orchid has a very special petal on its flower that is the same size and shape as a female bee. A male bee, searching for a female to **mate** with, is fooled by the bee orchid's petal, and lands on it. The orchid's pollen then rubs onto the bee and is carried by the bee to other bee orchids it may pollinate.

A bee orchid flower is dark and velvety, like a bumble bee. Dark colors are outlined by light colors so males can spot them easily.

The lower petal color is like a bee. It even has a false head and **antennae**.

14

The bee orchid is a champion copycat both in appearance and smell.

Perfume Power

Male and female bumble bees look very similar, so how can the bee orchid fool males into thinking their flowers are female bees? The answer is **pheromones**. These are special perfume chemicals. The bee orchid makes pheromones that match those made by female bumble bees to make sure a male bee visits.

Secret Stars

The rewardless orchid attracts hornets to pollinate its flowers. The pheromone it releases mimics one made by honeybees when they are alarmed. Honeybees are food for the hornets' young. Hornets visit the flowers expecting to find bees to hunt there!

15

Bamboo

Gardeners must wait with patience to watch their plants grow, unless they grow bamboo plants! Of all plants, the bamboo grows the most quickly. Some of the 1,200 types of bamboo can grow a staggering 35 inches (90 cm) each day. The tallest types can grow up to 130 feet (40 m) in 60 days!

Bamboo canes grow in segments. First, one stretches out and then the next, like the sections of a telescope.

Bamboo leaves grow between the segments of the plant. Branches with more leaves appear when the plant is at full height.

Underground Network

Bamboo can grow so quickly because of the plant's activity underground. The bamboo grows upward from a network of underground stems, called rhizomes, that have roots. The large network allows the plant to store and share its nutrients, sugar, and water equally among its canes.

The bamboo above ground relies on its underground network to help it grow fast.

Top Talent

For their size and weight, bamboo canes are incredibly strong. For this reason, they are often used in building works. They are even stronger than many types of steel and concrete. The canes' strength results from their tough walls of fibers that are held together with a strong natural glue.

17

Coconut

Coconut palms are trees that grow on beaches in tropical areas. Many grow from seeds that floated and drifted to land on ocean waves. The fruit of coconut trees fall on beaches and are washed into the sea. When the fruit wash up on another beach, they grow roots. The roots take hold in the ground and a new tree develops.

The so-called eyes on a coconut are the weaker spots on the seed through which a stem and leaves sprout.

The coconut fruit is the husk around the hard seed. This helps the seed to float and protects it from being damaged.

18

Tough Nut

Coconuts are incredibly tough seeds. The hard case protects the young plant, and its supply of food inside, from animals that want to eat it. Only animals such as coconut crabs have the strength to crack open one.

The coconut crab uses its giant claws to poke holes in coconuts. It even carries coconuts up trees and drops them on the ground to crack open the shells!

Top Talent

Coconuts also take top prize for the largest seeds amongst all plants. One type, called the coco-de-mer, which grows only on the Seychelles islands, has seeds that weigh up to 60 pounds (27 kg).

Giant Amazon Water Lily

Can you walk on water? Perhaps you could, on a bridge of giant Amazon water lilies! These record-breaking leaves are 8 feet (2.4 m) across and they could easily support the weight of a child, although we do not recommend you try it! The leaves float on the surface of the water, which allows the plant to get the sunlight it needs for photosynthesis.

Biggest Leaf

Tubes filled with air radiate like the spokes on a bicycle wheel on the bottom of the leaf. They help the leaf to stay afloat.

The top surface of a giant water lily leaf is smooth and rubbery.

Survival of the Biggest

Thorns on the bottom of the leaves of giant Amazon water lilies deter fish. Another survival tactic is to stop other water plants growing nearby and thereby taking the water lily's light. Each plant can grow 40 to 50 leaves, enough to completely cover a large area of a lake or a pond.

Fish think twice about tucking into water lily leaves because of their spikes.

Top Talent

Giant water lilies make sure they are pollinated by kidnapping beetles! The flowers open at night and release nectar to attract beetles. The beetles pollinate the plant, but then the flowers close, trapping the beetle. The flowers then release all their pollen over the beetle, before releasing it. The beetle then flies to other lilies and pollinates them with its pollen covering.

21

Bristlecone Pine

Bristlecone pines are named for their purple cones that have bristles on them.

Bristlecone pine trees are one of the oldest-living things on Earth. Some are known to be more than 3,000 years old and one is thought to be almost 5,000 years old. They grow in the mountains of the southwestern United States.

Bristlecone pines grow incredibly slowly so they do not use up too much energy.

Playing Dead

If bristlecone pines are damaged by fire or **drought**, much of the bark and the parts of the tree that carry water around it die. The tree looks dead, but it is actually saving energy and food so that it can survive until the next summer. Then, it suddenly bursts into life again, and produces new cones with new seeds.

Summers are short in the mountains, so bristlecone pines grow quickly in summer and rest in winter.

Top Talent

To find the age of a tree we count the number of growth rings inside its trunk. The rings tell us about Earth's past climate, too. Trees grow wide rings when it is wet and the soil is good, and narrow rings when it is dry and soil is poor. Even after the tree has died, bristlecone pine trunks last so long they can tell us what the climate was like 9,000 years ago!

Mesquite Tree

Deepest Root

It is a hard life for plants in the Sonoran Desert. It is very hot and dry and it rarely rains. However, the mesquite tree has an ingenious way of getting water to survive. Its roots grow quickly and stretch very deep to reach pockets of moisture underground. The longest recorded roots were more than 70 feet (20 m) long!

In times of drought the mesquite tree can lose its leaves to save water.

Mesquite trees vary in height but can grow to 30 feet (10 m) high.

Desert animals feed on the large seed cases that grow on mesquite trees.

Secret Stars

The tumboa plant found in southern African deserts has a unique tactic to get water. It has a very short stem and two long, tattered leaves that angle inward. Water from nighttime fog gathers on the leaves and trickles down toward the roots.

Back to Life

In some places, farmers worry that mesquite trees take water from the land that their crops could use. However, when they try to chop down the tree, they find that it simply grows back, again and again. This is because the roots of the mesquite tree can regenerate and grow new parts above ground. It makes the mesquite very hard to get rid of!

Jackfruit Tree

The jackfruit tree takes the prize for the plant that grows the largest fruit. This giant Asian tree grows 50 to 70 feet (15 to 20 m) tall. It has to be big and strong to hold up its vast fruits. Jackfruits can grow up to about 2 feet (60 cm) long and weigh up to about 40 pounds (18 kg). Imagine carrying that home from the store in your bag!

A jackfruit tree can produce around 700 fruits a year.

Jackfruits grow directly out of the trunk or branches.

When a jackfruit is ripe, it smells a little like pineapple. Its flesh tastes like a tangy banana.

Elephant Transport

When jackfruits are ripe their seeds are ready to grow. The tree needs to ensure the seeds grow someplace new so they do not compete with it for water and light. The ripe fruit gives off a scent elephants smell from far away. It takes an elephant days to digest jackfruits, so when it finally drops the seeds in its waste they are far from the parent tree.

Elephants help jackfruit trees spread their seeds.

Secret Stars

The spiky South Asian durian is another award-winning smelly fruit! The durian is famous for being the smelliest fruit in the world. Its odor is so bad that some airlines have banned people from taking the fruit on board their airplanes!

Amazing Adaptations

The stone plant's appearance disguises it to help it avoid being eaten by hungry animals.

Some plants are superstars because they have developed features to help them survive. This is called physical **adaptation**. For example, a palm tree's huge leaves help it capture the light it needs to make its own food. The shape and colors of the stone plant look like rocks, which disguises the plant.

Behavioral Adaptations

Some adaptations are behavioral. These are things that plants do to survive. Tulips and some other flowers open their petals in the daytime but close them at night. This stops their precious pollen from becoming wet and heavy with dew. The sensitive plant also has leaves that fold up when touched. This protects it from animals that try to eat it.

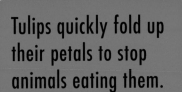

Tulips quickly fold up their petals to stop animals eating them.

Top Talent

When plants use energy from the Sun to make food in their leaves, they help people, too. Not only do we need plants for food, but in the process of photosynthesis, plants also take in carbon dioxide and release oxygen. Carbon dioxide is a gas that is bad for humans in large amounts. Oxygen is the gas that people and other animals need to breathe to live.

29

Glossary

adaptation (a-dap-TAY-shun) A feature or way of behaving that helps an animal survive.

antennae (an-TEH-nee) Sense organs located on the front of an insect's head.

cones (KOHNZ) Egg-shaped parts of evergreen trees that hold the plants' seeds.

digest (dy-JEST) To break down food.

drought (DROWT) A long period of time without rain.

mate (MAYT) To reproduce.

nectar (NEK-tur) The sweet, sugary juice flowers make.

nutrients (NOO-tree-ents) The substances living things take in or eat to help them live and grow.

pheromones (FER-uh-mohnz) Substances that organisms release to signal other organisms.

pollen (PAH-lin) A powder produced by the male parts of a flower.

pollinate (PAH-luh-nayt) When pollen is carried from one flower to the female parts of another flower to make seeds grow there.

sap (SAP) The watery fluid that carries food and other substances around a plant.

seeds (SEEDZ) The parts that a plant produces to grow into new plants like itself.

stems (STEMZ) The parts of a plant that hold up its leaves and flowers.

Further Reading

Gould, Margee. *Giant Plants*. The Strangest Plants on
Earth. New York: PowerKids Press, 2012.

Gray, Leon. *Plant Classification*. Life Science Stories.
New York: Gareth Stevens, 2013.

Waldron, Melanie. *Seeds and Fruits*. Plant Parts.
Mankato, MN: Capstone Press, 2014.

Websites

Due to the changing nature of Internet links, PowerKids
Press has developed an online list of websites related to
the subject of this book. This site is updated regularly.
Please use this link to access the list:
www.powerkidslinks.com/ngt/plant/

Index

A

adaptations, 28–29

B

bark, 6–7, 12–13, 23
branches, 6, 12, 16, 26

C

cacti, 4, 13
carbon dioxide, 4, 29
chlorophyll, 4
climate, 23
coco-de-mer, 19
cones, 4, 7, 22–23

D

desert, 4, 24–25
dragon's blood tree, 5
drought, 23–24

F

fires, 7, 12, 23
flowers, 4, 8–9, 14–15,
    21, 29

G

giant saguaro, 13
giant sequoias, 7
growth rings, 23

I

insects, 9–11

L

leaves, 4, 6, 8, 10–11, 16,
    18, 20–21, 24–25,
    28–29

N

nectar, 11, 21
nutrients, 6–8, 10–11, 17

P

petal, 14, 29
pheromones, 15
photosynthesis, 4, 20, 29
pitcher plants, 11
pollen, 9, 14, 21, 29
pollinate, 9, 14–15, 21

R

rewardless orchid, 15
rhizomes, 17
roots, 4, 6–7, 17–18,
    24–25

S

sap, 5
seeds, 4, 7–9, 13, 18–19,
    23–24, 27
sensitive plant, 29
stems, 4, 17–18, 25
stone plant, 28
sugar, 4, 17

T

thorns, 21
titan arum, 9
trees, 4–7, 12–13, 18–19,
    22–28
trunk, 5, 12–13, 23, 26
tulips, 29

W

water, 4, 7, 12–13, 17–18,
    20, 23–25, 27